The Really Easy Brass Series

General Editor: John Ridgeon

The *Really* Easy Tenor Horn Book

Very first solos for horn/soprano cornet in E♭
with piano accompaniment

Leslie Pearson

Faber Music Limited
London

2

1. Russian Dance

L.P.

2. Nobilmente

L.P.

3. Lament

L.P.

GI

4. Minuet in C

George Frederic Handel
arr. L.P.

5. Moto perpetuo

L.P.

6

6. Leap-frog

L.P.

7. Le Petit Rien

François Couperin
arr. L.P.

8. Rag Trade

L.P.

9. Seven-up

L.P.

The Really Easy Brass Series
General Editor: John Ridgeon

The *Really* Easy Tenor Horn Book

Very first solos for horn/soprano cornet in E♭
with piano accompaniment

Leslie Pearson

Faber Music Limited
London

Preface

You need only be able to play a few notes on the tenor horn (or soprano cornet) to make music. The nine little pieces in this book have been written and selected with beginners in mind, but within the technical limitations this imposes there is plenty of scope for musical interest. The pieces are arranged progressively, so as well as musical satisfaction you can have the pleasure of hearing the step-by-step improvement in your playing. The piano accompaniments have been kept as simple as possible.

© 1987 by Faber Music Ltd
First published in 1987 by Faber Music Ltd
3 Queen Square London WC1N 3AU
Music drawn by Lincoln Castle Music
Cover illustration by Penny Dann
Cover design by M & S Tucker
Printed in England by Caligraving Ltd

Contents

1. Russian Dance

L.P.

2. Nobilmente

L.P.

3. Lament

L.P.

6

4. Minuet in C

George Frederic Handel
arr. L.P.

5. Moto perpetuo

L.P.

6. Leap-frog

L.P.

poco rit.   a tempo

7. Le Petit Rien

François Couperin
arr. L.P.

8. Rag Trade

L.P.

9. Seven-up

L.P.

D.C. al 🔷 poi al Coda

CODA